1903 · THE WORLD'S FIRST AIRPLANE

ROBERT QUACKENBUSH

# TAKE ME OUT TO THE AIRFIELD!

## HOW THE WRIGHT BROTHERS INVENTED THE AIRPLANE

PARENTS' MAGAZINE PRESS · NEW YORK.

*For my brother*
*Roy E. Quackenbush*
*with thanks and appreciation,*
*and for my son, Piet*

*Library of Congress Cataloging in Publication Data*
Quackenbush, Robert M.
    Take me out to the airfield!
    SUMMARY: A picture-book biography of the Wright brothers who made the first successful motor-powered flight in the history of mankind.
    1. Wright, Orville, 1871-1948—Juvenile literature. 2. Wright, Wilbur, 1867-1912—Juvenile literature. [1. Wright, Orville, 1871-1948. 2. Wright, Wilbur, 1867-1912. 3. Aeronautics—Biography]
I. Title. TL540.W7Q3 629.13′092′4 [B] [920] 76-2558
ISBN 0-8193-0879-X ISBN 0-8193-0880-3 lib. bdg.

# PROLOGUE

*Sung to "Take Me Out to the Ball Game!"*

*Take me out to the airfield!*
*Tell me all about planes!*
*Who invented them? How was it done?*
*I want to know who flew the first one.*
*Tell, please, tell me about planes.*
*How did they get in the sky?*
*With a one, two, three tell me now—*
*How we learned to fly!*

 1877 · THE BROTHERS BUILD THEIR OWN TOYS

There were once two brothers named Wilbur and Orville Wright. Wilbur was four years older than Orville. The boys' father was a minister. Since there were three other children in the Wright family, there was seldom money left over to buy toys. But Wilbur and Orville didn't mind. Their mother, whose father had been a wagon builder, taught them how to use tools. So the brothers made their own toys.

The minister was proud of his two clever sons. One day, when Wilbur was eleven and Orville seven, he brought home a surprise. He knew they would like it.

His present was a toy made with a rubber band and a propeller. When the boys wound the propeller and let the toy leave their hands—zip! zip!—it flew up in the air.

Wilbur and Orville couldn't believe their eyes. It was the first time they had seen a toy that could fly.

1878 · THE BROTHERS RECEIVE A PRESENT

1879 · THE BROTHERS SELL THEIR KITES

From that day on, the two brothers dreamed of flying. They made copies of their present. They even tried to build a big one, but it was too heavy to leave the ground. So they began making kites. The brothers flew their kites and pretended they were flying, too.

When other children saw the kites, they wanted to buy them. So Orville and Wilbur began selling their kites. Soon they were building other things, like mechanical toys, which they also sold.

By the time they grew up, the brothers had saved enough money to open a bicycle repair shop. But behind their shop, they still made kites and studied science in their free time. They had not given up the idea of flying.

One day, Wilbur read in the newspaper about a German engineer who had invented a man-carrying kite called a glider. Studying the flight of birds, this engineer had built his glider with wings shaped like bird wings—slightly curved at the top. He balanced his glider in the air by moving his body or kicking his legs as he flew. Wilbur couldn't believe that a big glider could be safely controlled simply by a man's shifting his own weight.

1894 • OTTO LILIETHAL'S GLIDER

1899 · THE BROTHERS WATCH BUZZARDS FLYING

Wilbur was right. One day, a gust of wind overturned the German glider. Though the engineer kicked with all his might, he could not right it. He fell to his death. Still, Orville and Wilbur thought that Lilienthal's idea of watching birds fly was a good one. Whenever they had the time, the brothers now bicycled to the countryside to watch buzzards flying. They also read the work of Octave Chanute, an American engineer who had built gliders, and Wilbur began to correspond with him. Chanute encouraged the brothers to experiment with human flight.

While watching birds, Orville noticed how well they were able to glide and turn in the sky, keeping themselves balanced in the wind. Their bodies seemed not to move at all. Instead, it looked as though the buzzards twisted the back edge of one wing downward and the back edge of the other upward. Could this be the answer to controlled flight?

Soon after Orville's discovery, Wilbur found a long empty box in the shop. When he put one hand at each end and turned the box in opposite directions, he found that it twisted like the buzzard's wings in flight. He realized that a kite could be built to do this same sort of twisting in the air.

The brothers made a new kite to test the discovery. This kite had two wings. They were five feet long and set one over the other with wooden struts. Each wing was still curved at the top like the German glider, but the wings also had wires and pullies attached to make them twist (or warp) in the air. The brothers could control this warping from the ground by moving two sticks with cords extending from them to the tips of each wing. Wilbur took the new kite to a field for testing. When it rose high in the air, he pulled first one stick and then the other to warp the wings. The kite flew as balanced as a buzzard in the wind!

1899 · WILBUR FLIES THE BROTHERS' WING KITE

1900 · THE BROTHERS BUILD A GLIDER.

Wilbur rushed back to the shop with the good news. Now the brothers could try to build their own man-sized glider.

All that year they worked on it. By September, 1900, their glider was ready for a test flight. Orville and Wilbur decided to take it to Kitty Hawk, a sandy beach off the coast of North Carolina, where the winds were always low and steady.

The glider was packed in crates, and Wilbur boarded a train with his precious cargo. Orville would follow when the shop was less busy.

When Wilbur reached the coast of North Carolina, he set sail for Kitty Hawk in a small fishing boat. Halfway there, the wind began blowing at gale force. The boat almost sank.

When Wilbur finally got to Kitty Hawk, he set up a tent in some sand dunes near the postmaster's house. He began putting the glider together. Orville came two weeks later to help.

At last, everything was ready. The glider had two wings like the kite, but they were more than three times as long. Extending from poles at the front of the glider, a tiny wing had been added as a kind of elevator. It could be tipped and help the glider to go up or down. There was also a place in the middle of the main bottom wing for the pilot. He rode, lying face down, so that he could work the elevator and wing controls.

When they tested the glider, the brothers found that it could not be flown higher than fifteen feet or it would teeter dangerously. It couldn't fly very far either—or turn. Only the wing – warping invention seemed sound. Something else was needed.

Discouraged, the brothers headed home. They left their first glider with the postmaster to be used for firewood!

1900 · THE BROTHERS WONDER WHY THEIR GLIDER WON'T FLY WELL

Back home, the brothers tried to figure out what was wrong. They built a heavier glider with still longer wings, but less of a top curve.

The next summer, Orville and Wilbur returned to Kitty Hawk. They launched their second glider from a high sand dune in the Kill Devil Hills. This glider made a flight of 389 feet, but it still couldn't fly very high. And once, when Wilbur tried to turn it, the left wing dropped too far and brushed the sand. The glider crashed!

Luckily, Wilbur wasn't badly hurt, but he was disappointed and discouraged. On the train going home, he said sadly, "Man will not fly in a thousand years." Orville had more hope. He suggested that they build a wind tunnel to check Lilienthal's figures, which they had been using for the glider's weight and wing size.

WHAT'S A WIND TUNNEL?

A LONG WOODEN BOX WITH A FAN AT ONE END AND TINY WING MODELS AT THE OTHER. WHEN THE FAN GOES ON, THE WINGS LIFT.

CLEVER!

1901 · THE BROTHERS' GLIDER CRASHES

1902 · THE BROTHERS BUILD A WIND TUNNEL

The wind tunnel experiments showed that Lilienthal's figures were not right! From then on, the brothers trusted only their own. After a thousand readings, using more than two hundred tiny wing models, they went to work on a new glider.

This glider had still longer, narrower wings and even less of a top curve. In addition, a tailpiece was added for balance. After a few test flights at Kitty Hawk in October, 1902, the tail was made to swing right or left, like a rudder. Now the glider could turn, because the rudder helped to balance it during wing – warping. And the glider could also keep steady in many different winds. The magic door to controlled flight by man in a heavier-than-air craft had been opened.

The brothers made hundreds of perfect glides up to distances of 622 feet. Orville and Wilbur became birdmen at last!

1902 • WILBUR TAKES A HIGH RIDE IN THE PERFECTED GLIDER

THE MAJOR PROBLEMS OF HUMAN FLIGHT HAVE BEEN SOLVED

The Wright brothers' successful glider made them the first inventors ready for powered flight. All they needed was a machine that could fly under its own power, without depending on the wind.

A year later, a new machine with a motor of their own design was finished and ready to be tested at Kitty Hawk. The Wrights called it the *Flyer.* Wilbur tossed a coin to decide who would be the first to try. He won! But when the *Flyer* was set in motion on a wooden rail that stretched down a slope, it made a bad start. Less than four seconds after take-off, it landed hard and was damaged.

Four days later, the brothers were ready to try again. This time, it was Orville's turn. The motor was started and the *Flyer* rolled forward. It rose ten feet in the air and kept on flying. In twelve seconds, it went 120 feet! Three more flights that day went up to 850 feet in 59 seconds. These four tests were the first successful flights of an airplane in the history of the world!

DECEMBER 13, 1903 · THE BROTHERS FLIP A COIN

DECEMBER 17, 1903 · THE WORLD'S FIRST SUCCESSFUL AIRPLANE FLIGHTS

By 1908, enough people had seen or heard of the brothers' triumph, so that orders began to come for the Wrights' *Flyer.* The brothers became rich and famous as they worked here and abroad setting up factories and pilot-training schools.

In 1910, Wilbur and Orville flew together for the first time in a two-man *Flyer* with upright seats. Afterwards, Orville took their father for a ride. "Higher! Higher!" the old minister shouted in the spirit of his two sons.

But not even the brothers ever dreamt how important their invention would be. Today, planes that move faster than the speed of sound can fly from one end of the earth to the other within a single day.

The brothers' patience and hard work was rewarded. Their *Flyer* was possibly the greatest single invention in the history of mankind.

1 styrofoam meat tray (the smooth kind)      1 dime
   or, 2 styrofoam egg carton tops      Scissors
Tape      Pencil
Flat wooden toothpicks      Paper
White glue      Carbon paper

1. Trace or copy the pattern. Put carbon paper under your drawing and trace it onto the styrofoam. (Remember to trace two wings, two elevators, and two rudders.)

2. Cut out all the parts. Shape the wings and elevators by cutting along the dotted lines.

3. Push toothpicks, lengthwise, through the center of each rudder. Glue each rudder upright at one end of the body—one to the right edge and the other to the left. Then glue on the rudder top.

4. Glue the first wing to the center of the body. Dip 18 toothpick ends in glue and place the toothpicks upright on the dot marks. Dab glue on the toothpick tops and lay the second wing carefully on them, using the dots as a guide. Cut a toothpick in half and glue one piece each to two middle toothpicks (as shown)—to look like propellers.

5. At the other end of the body, glue the elevator. Dip five toothpick ends in glue and place the toothpicks upright on the dot marks. Dab glue on the tops and place the second elevator on them.

6. Tape dime to the bottom of the *Flyer* between the wing and the elevator.

7. Wait for glue to dry. Cut off with scissors any toothpick ends that stick up. Now you are ready for take-off! Kneel down and fly your model—nice and low, just like the Wright brothers flew their first *Flyer*!

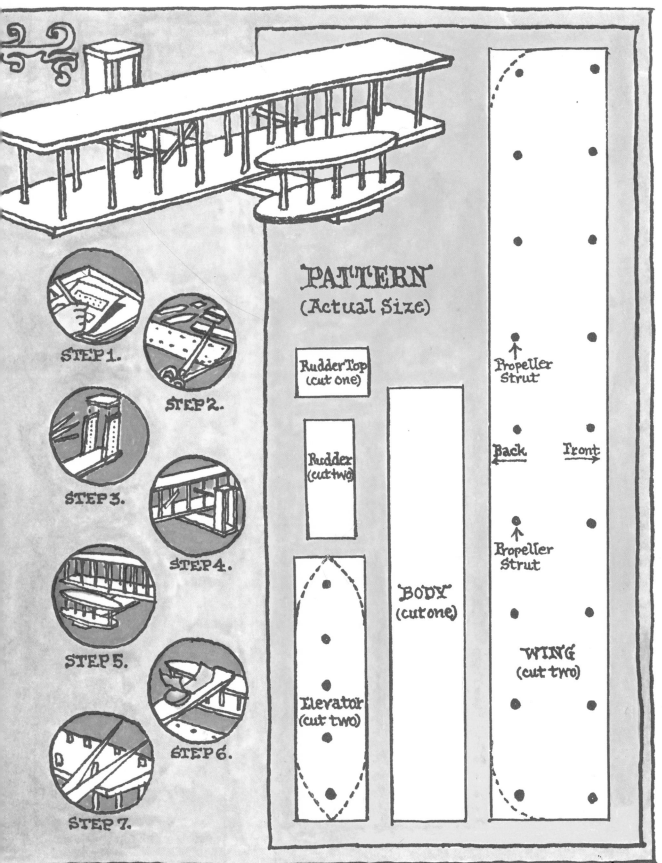

STEP 1.

STEP 2.

STEP 3.

STEP 4.

STEP 5.

STEP 6.

STEP 7.

# PATTERN
## (Actual Size)

Rudder Top
(cut one)

Rudder
(cut two)

Elevator
(cut two)

BODY
(cut one)

Propeller
Strut

Back     Front

Propeller
Strut

WING
(cut two)

Designed by Roy E. Quackenbush

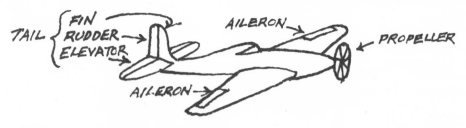

# HOW AN AIRPLANE FLIES

As an airplane moves forward, air slips over and under the wings. The air that goes over the curved top of the wing moves faster than the air that goes under the straight bottom of the wing. The difference in air pressure that results—much less on top than underneath the wing—is what lifts an airplane up into the sky. But, as the Wright brothers discovered, other things are necessary in order for an airplane to fly—and to stay balanced once in the air. So the brothers invented wing warping, which helped the airplane tip sideways and to turn; an elevator to help it move lower or higher; a rudder which helped it turn smoothly; propellers to pull it through the air; and a motor to give it power. All these things work together to enable an airplane to fly and stay balanced in the air.

Modern airplanes still use all the brothers' discoveries. But ailerons (small, moveable panels at the outer tips of the wings) have now simplified wing warping.

The elevator, which moves up and down, and the rudder, which moves left and right, are both at the tail of today's airplane and are controlled from the cockpit. Many planes are now *pushed* through the air by jet propulsion instead of being *pulled* through the air by propellers. Even so, the Wright brothers' three basic controls—wing warping, the elevator, and the rudder—remain vital to flight.

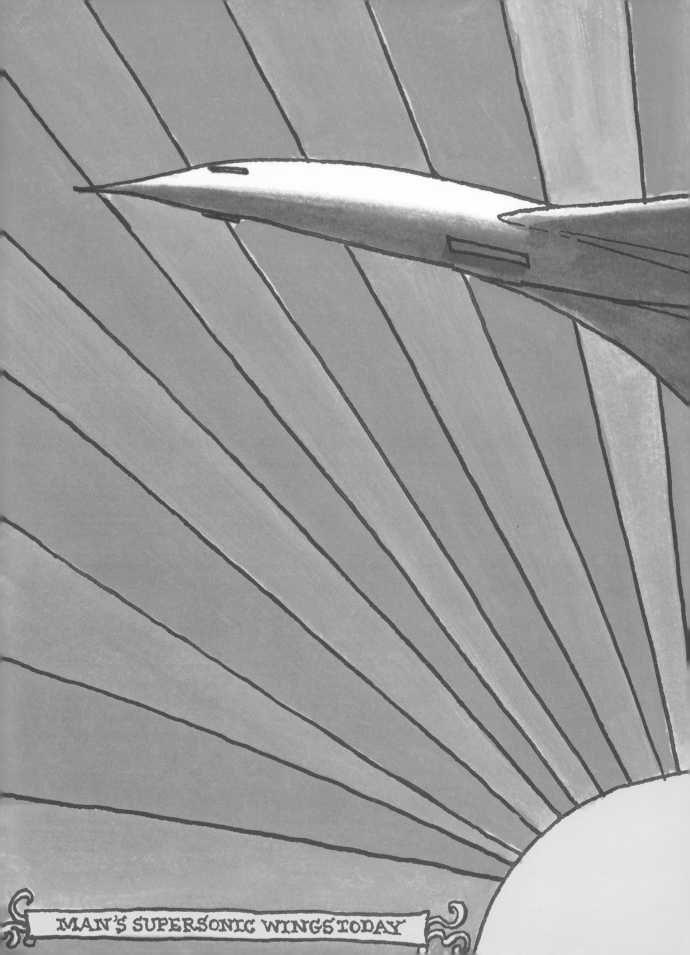

MAN'S SUPERSONIC WINGS TODAY

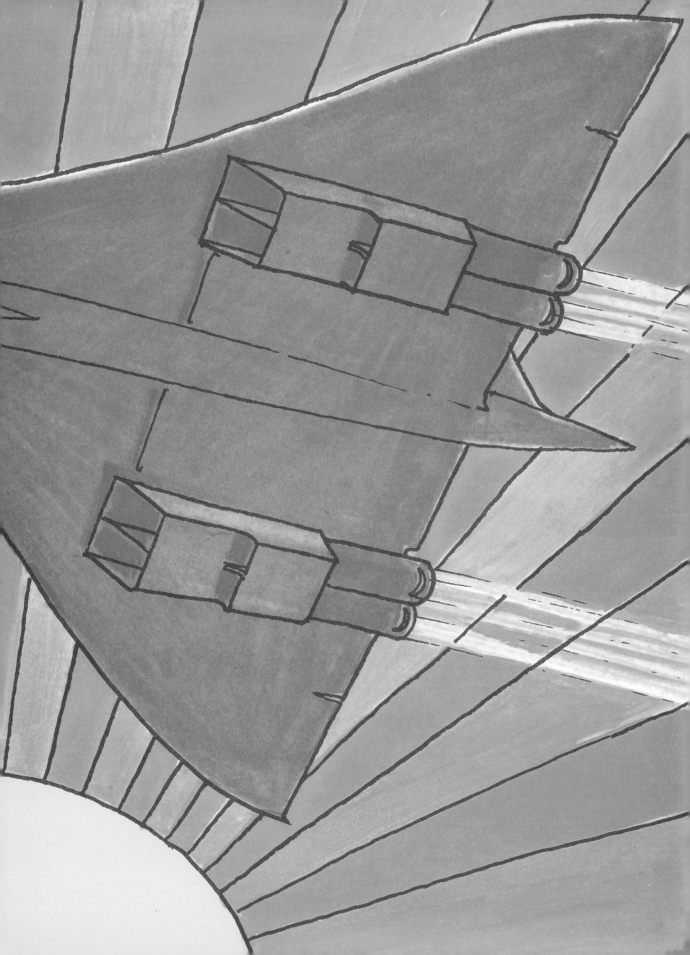